QUAKERS

Peter Furtado

SHIRE PUBLICATIONS

Published in Great Britain in 2013 by Shire Publications Ltd, Midland House, West Way, Botley, Oxford OX2 0PH, United Kingdom.

43-01 21st Street, Suite 220B, Long Island City, NY 11101, USA.

E-mail: shire@shirebooks.co.uk   www.shirebooks.co.uk

© 2013 Peter Furtado.

Every attempt has been made by the Publishers to secure the appropriate permissions for materials reproduced in this book. If there has been any oversight we will be happy to rectify the situation and a written submission should be made to the Publishers.

A CIP catalogue record for this book is available from the British Library.

Shire Library no. 752.   ISBN-13: 978 0 74781 250 0

Peter Furtado has asserted his right under the Copyright, Designs and Patents Act, 1988, to be identified as the author of this book.

Designed by Ken Vail Graphic Design and typeset in Perpetua and Gill Sans.

Printed in China through Worldprint Ltd.

13 14 15 16 17   10 9 8 7 6 5 4 3 2 1

COVER IMAGE
The Marriage of William Penn and Hannah Callowhill at the Friends' Meeting House, The Friary, Bristol, 1696. Ernest Board, 1916.

TITLE PAGE IMAGE
George Fox, founder of the Quakers, who is traditionally said to have worn a wide-brimmed hat, 'leather breeches and shaggy, shaggy locks'.

CONTENTS PAGE IMAGE
A dramatised nineteenth-century view of George Fox refusing to swear the Oath of Allegiance, asserting that to swear an oath implies a lesser standard of truth on other occasions.

ACKNOWLEDGEMENTS
Every effort has been made to trace the copyright holders of the illustrations used in this book. I would like to thank the people who have allowed me to use illustrations, which are acknowledged as follows:

Alamy, 44 (bottom), 46, 47; Andrew Riley, page 6; Brighton Friends meeting, pages 23 (top), 27; Bristol Museum and Art Gallery, front cover; Corbis, page 37 (top); Friends House Library, pages 8–9, 11 (bottom), 14, 17, 18, 23 (bottom), 26 (right), 33, 35, 36, 42–3, 48 (bottom left), 49, 50; Greenpeace/Robert Keziere, page 5; Library of Congress, pages 20, 25, 28, 40 (bottom); Look and Learn/The Bridgeman Art Library, page 58 (right); National Portrait Gallery, page 11 (top), 50; Philadelphia Museum of Art, Pennsylvania, PA, USA/The Bridgeman Art Library, page 59; Quaker Tapestry, pages 4, 51, 62; Sarah Lasenby, pages 30 (bottom), 61 (bottom); Selly Oak Museum, page 56; Swarthmore College, page 30 (top); Valerie Hurwitz, page 60. All other images are from the author's collection.

Shire Publications is supporting the Woodland Trust, the UK's leading woodland conservation charity, by funding the dedication of trees.

CONTENTS

WHO ARE THE QUAKERS?

IF QUAKERS were not strictly pacifist, they could be described as consistently 'punching above their weight'. A small sect – currently fewer than 20,000 members in the UK and just 100,000 in the US – has produced a disproportionate number of eminent thinkers, scientists and businessmen, as well as radical ideas that go on to be adopted by the mainstream. Among their number can be counted two US presidents (and one First Lady), several Nobel prize-winners, writers, actors and musicians, philanthropists, reformers, campaigners, educators, economists … the list goes on and on.

Quakers have affected daily life in other ways. They are associated with some of the world's best-known consumer brands, especially for confectionery (Cadbury's, Rowntree's and Fry's), although the jovial Quaker on the familiar

The 'divine light', as represented in one of the seventy-seven panels of the Quaker Tapestry, created in the 1980s and '90s, and now in a museum in Kendal. More than 4,000 men, women and children in fifteen countries had a hand in its creation.

THE RELIGIOUS SOCIETY of FRIENDS "might be thought of as a prism through which the DIVINE LIGHT passes to become visible in a spectrum of many colours; many more in their richness than words alone can express" Faith + Practice

Irving and Dorothy Stowe, two of the founders of the environmental direct-action campaigning group Greenpeace, were greatly influenced by Quakerism. The first voyage on the ship *Greenpeace* was to stop nuclear testing in the Pacific in 1971.

oats package is a marketing invention rather than a historical individual. It is true, though, that a Quaker developed the board game Monopoly (as an educational activity to teach the perils of landlordism).

Quakers have been at the forefront of campaigns for peace and social justice all around the world. Once the leaders of the fight against slavery on three continents, in recent decades they have worked tirelessly with the United Nations and many other international bodies, NGOs and charities seeking to bring an end to the world's most intractable conflicts, fighting poverty, campaigning against war and helping those whose lives are blighted by violence, whatever its source.

While it is not hard to point to what Quakers do, and the difference they have made to the world, it is much more difficult to pin down what Quakers believe. We can state, simply, what Quakers are: they are members of the Religious Society of Friends, a group that emerged in mid-seventeenth-century England as a fresh and personal expression of the teaching of Christ and the God of the Bible. It was founded by a shoemaker from Leicestershire, George Fox, who preached that every man, woman and child could have a direct experience of 'God within' simply by listening – and thus priests, hierarchies, sacraments or rituals all served to obstruct this experience. He also urged people to 'tremble in the face of the Lord' – a phrase taken up by a hostile judge in 1650 who jeered at Fox and his followers as 'Quakers'. The name stuck.

George Fox also refused to impose a hierarchy or formal leadership on his Society, nor was there any kind of creed that a Quaker had to sign up to – with the result that many Quakers no longer see themselves as Christians in the sense of believing in the saving power of the resurrection of Christ. Instead there is a confusing diversity of belief, practice and organisation within Quakerism. In some countries there is a single body that represents most Quakers living there (in Britain this is known as 'Britain Yearly Meeting'); but elsewhere there may be many such Yearly Meetings, representing geographical, historical or theological diversity: in the United States alone there are more than thirty. As a result, modern Quakers' beliefs are very varied, as are the various churches — Meetings — around the world. Some Quakers are socially conservative evangelical Christians; others are liberal in politics and plural in belief — with Quaker Jews, Buddhists and Muslims, as well as Quaker theists (universalists) and even Quaker atheists, standing alongside those who recognise the Christian God that Fox taught. Consecrated churches are rejected, and in earlier times Quakers resisted the expectation that they would pay tithes to finance the 'steeple-house' (church) and its 'professor' (priest). Nevertheless, Quakers sometimes have professional or paid ministers, and in some traditions these are crucial to the life of their church.

The emphasis on the inner light, on the direct experience of God, led early Quakers to adopt a unique form of worship. Instead of services, they held 'Meetings for Worship', sitting in silence (broken by occasional spontaneous

Brigflatts Meeting House, in Cumbria, built in 1675, is typical of the modest Quaker Meeting Houses of Britain and New England. Unlike churches, Meeting Houses are not considered more sanctified places than anywhere else.

Left: A French view of
a Quaker Meeting in the
very early eighteenth century,
showing a woman preaching
from the balcony.

Below: William Penn was a
leading Quaker propagandist
in the 1670s, and established
the US state of Pennsylvania
with an idealistic constitution
in the 1680s.

'ministries' from members), waiting and listening for the word of
God to show the way forward. Sitting in silence is not universal,
however: some Quaker Meetings have 'structured services'
that include hymns, psalms and prayers. Yet sitting together in
expectant silence is cherished by Quakers across the globe,
and is often seen as the distinctively Quaker practice.

Quakers apply similar principles to the running of
their affairs. Business meetings are known as 'Meetings
for Worship for Business', and are conducted in
silence, broken by measured interventions.
No votes are taken and no decisions
made until there is a sense of the will
of God in the room. This sense is
meticulously summed up in a written
minute that is agreed by the whole meeting. The process,
which can admittedly be slow, is inclusive and often creative.

Instead of a formal creed, Quakers share an
understanding, ethic and code of conduct, which is summed
up in two volumes – *Advices and Queries*, a slim set of
aphorisms and questions which are regularly read and
discussed, and the *Book of Discipline*, which sets out
the regulations for the 'right ordering' (proper
running) of the Meeting and includes many
short, inspirational quotations collected from
Quakers over the centuries. Neither volume
is set in stone, but is regularly reviewed and updated a
process of true collaboration involving all who wish to take part.

The mysterious communion of silent Meeting for Worship was captured in this popular painting, *Presence in the Midst* by Doyle Penrose, in the early twentieth century.

Left: The portrait of prison reformer Elizabeth Fry has been reproduced on Bank of England £5 notes since 2001.

The present book aims to set out the world of the Quakers by exploring the origins of the sect in the aftermath of the English Civil War and its persecution under the Restoration; how it spread to the Americas; and how on both sides of the Atlantic the ideas grew and changed through the succeeding centuries, to the diversity, and the worldwide reach, of today.

However, an historical approach cannot do justice to a Society that is built on the inner life of its members; so the heart of the book explores the meaning of Quakerism, and the conviction that has led so many into hardship and danger, by examining its core insights. These are known as 'testimonies' – and the major Quaker testimonies form the essence of what unifies Quakers worldwide.

Central among these is the peace testimony, originally expressed in 1660 in the following words: 'All bloody principles and practices we do utterly deny, with all outward wars & strife, and fightings with outward weapons, for any end or under any pretence whatsoever.' The urge to bear witness to this central insight of the message of Christ has seen Quakers consistently refuse to fight and instead to work for peace and reconciliation.

The testimony of justice, equality and community expresses the sense that every person has 'that of God' within and so deserves to be approached with absolute equality.

The testimony of truth and integrity gave rise to a refusal to swear oaths – which led many early Quakers into conflict with the authorities – but eventually gave Quakers a reputation for being honest businessmen and led them to establish some of the most successful enterprises of the eighteenth and nineteenth centuries.

The testimony of simplicity led Quakers to live and dress plainly, avoiding ostentation, but also to reject excessive consumerism and the unsustainable use of natural resources. This was once linked to a testimony 'of times and seasons', which denied that any days in the calendar were more 'holy' than others, and so rejected religious festivals. Today the testimony of simplicity is more closely linked with a newly emerging testimony of the earth and the environment, which seeks to restore harmony between people and the planet.

A Meeting of
'weighty Friends'
in 1699, presided
over by George
Whitehead, who
is buried in Bunhill
Fields, London, next
to George Fox.

Below: Friends
House in Euston
Square, London,
is the headquarters
of Britain Yearly
Meeting. The
architect's drawing
placed in it a more
secluded setting
than the crowded
Euston Road of the
twenty-first century.

THE ORIGINS OF
QUAKERISM

THE ESSENTIAL INSIGHT of George Fox, that every individual has direct and personal access to the light and love of God, was both a culmination of the Puritan movement, and a transcendence of it. No longer was society divided between the priests and the laity, between the elect and the damned, or even between men and women. All were equal before God – and should be equal on earth as well. It was a radical message, one suited for the revolutionary times in which Fox lived.

Brought up in a Puritan household, in the late 1640s the young Fox went on a literal and spiritual journey through an England torn by civil war. He fell into a deep depression, which he described vividly:

> But as I had forsaken the priests, so I left the separate preachers also, and those esteemed the most experienced people; for I saw there was none among them all that could speak to my condition. And when all my hopes in them and in all men were gone, so that I had nothing outwardly to help me, nor could tell what to do, then, oh, then, I heard a voice which said, 'There is one, even Christ Jesus, that can speak to thy condition'; and when I heard it my heart did leap for joy …
>
> I saw also that there was an ocean of darkness and death; but an infinite ocean of light and love, which flowed over the ocean of darkness. In that also I saw the infinite love of God, and I had great openings …

Firbank Fell, in Cumbria, where George Fox preached to one thousand people and effectively began the Society of Friends.

By the early 1650s, Fox was building a group of followers, and from 1652 – when he had a vision on Pendle Hill, Lancashire, of an unstoppable mass movement – the message was spread through a group of travelling preachers, who became known as the Valiant Sixty. Several were women; some were very young. They won a ready hearing, especially among tradesmen and craftsmen of the north of England, and then more widely, in an England whose cultural and political moorings had been lost in the recent civil wars and aftermath. Fox and his followers proclaimed their message with great insistence, preaching that the Last Judgement was imminent and they were the true saints. They challenged the old norms in dramatic fashion: interrupting church services to denounce the false preaching of the 'hireling priests'; walking naked through the marketplace (as the young Elizabeth Fletcher did in Oxford in 1654, 'a sign against that hypocritical profession they then made there, being then Presbyterians and Independents, which confession she told them the Lord would strip them of, so that their nakedness should appear' – she was nearly killed by the 'black tribe of scholars' for her pains); refusing to pay tithes; and refusing to bury their dead in hallowed ground. In a notorious incident in 1656 the leading Quaker James Nayler re-enacted Christ's entry into Jerusalem, riding into Bristol on a horse.

This board game, entitled 'The Quaker Game, 1652 country' commemorates George Fox's visit to northern Lancashire and Cumbria, the decisive moment in the foundation of the Quaker movement.

13

George Fox proclaimed his message in a striking manner, as here, walking barefoot through the marketplace, proclaiming 'woe to the bloody city of Lichfield'. Engraving by Robert Spence.

Reactions were mixed. Many Quakers, including Fox himself, were repeatedly flung into jail – and Nayler was branded and had his tongue bored for his blasphemy – yet the Lord Protector Oliver Cromwell himself showed some sympathy for Fox's message, if not his methods. By the end of the 1650s, in some parts of England almost a tenth of the population was proclaiming Quaker sympathies. They took the name 'Friends' from a passage in the Bible where Jesus told his followers, 'I have called you friends, for all that I have heard from my Father I have made known to you.' Some were former political radicals – men like the Leveller and proto-democrat John Lilburne or the former Digger Gerard Winstanley – but many others were tradespeople and gentry who were not apparently seeking a direct challenge to the political and social order, but were inspired by the optimistic teachings.

In 1660 the Restoration of the Stuarts – and with them the established Church of England – dashed Fox's hope that the Society of Friends might become the main church in the country. Far from it, as Parliament

introduced a strict penal code aimed at all those religious radicals on whom were blamed the woes of the previous two decades. Between 1661 and 1664, a series of acts of Parliament ejected non-conformists from town corporations, banned non-Anglican religious meetings of five or more people and then banned non-conformist ministers from coming within five miles of any town. The Quakers suffered from all these, as well as, from 1662, an act specifically aimed at them: 'preventing the Mischeifs [sic] and Dangers that may arise by certaine Persons called Quakers and others refusing to take lawfull Oaths'.

This vindictive law makes evident the fear that the established order had for the Quaker message – and the following three decades were a time of almost continual persecution, with meetings broken up violently, many Quakers arrested and suffering repeated periods in prison, and hundreds dying there. George Fox's journal provides a vivid, day-by-day (and, almost literally, blow-by-blow) account of the arguments and persecution he himself endured as he preached his faith around the country. Some were attacked for petty but symbolic offences – imprisonment for opening a shop on Christmas Day, for example.

Nevertheless, the faith survived, and this was its heroic phase from which many stories and personalities survive. Quakers tried to meet openly, but became familiar with ways of combating the legal attacks on them. If they were not permitted to meet for worship in houses, they would meet in the street. On one occasion the entire adult Quaker population of Reading was thrown into gaol; their children, though, continued to worship in a barn, despite regular beatings, until their parents were released.

Quakers received some protection from supporters at court, not least from

Above: James Nayler having his tongue bored as part of the punishment imposed by Parliament for his apparent blasphemy in riding into Bristol in 1656 in emulation of Jesus.

Left: A seventeenth-century drawing of a Quaker, wearing a typical broad-brimmed hat.

William Penn, who himself had suffered imprisonment more than once – firstly spending a year in the Tower for having denied the Trinity, and secondly when he and others were arrested for holding a meeting in Gracechurch Street in London; the jury at their trial refused to convict them, and was itself gaoled and starved by the judge for several days. An outcry forced him to back down, thereby establishing the enduring tradition that juries cannot be suborned by judges. Penn became an unlikely favourite of the king, and on several occasions was able to intercede successfully on behalf of his co-religionists.

Surviving the years of persecution was in part achieved through the establishment of some Quaker institutions that still endure. First was a system of local 'Monthly Meetings' reporting to regional 'Quarterly Meetings' and ultimately to a 'London Yearly Meeting', which served as the ultimate decision-making body of the Society. (This terminology endured until very recently.) One offshoot of London Yearly Meeting was the establishment in 1675 of a meeting at which each Monthly Meeting reported the deaths, imprisonment and other suffering it had endured, and which took action to seek redress and religious toleration. This became known as the 'Meeting for Sufferings', and it still exists as the central executive arm of the Society of Friends in Britain.

A detail of the *Book of Sufferings* of 1691, detailing the imprisonment of Quakers in Huntingdonshire.

During these years too, the Quakers' distinctive business method was clarified, in which members met in silence to discern the will of God and kept careful written minutes of all their proceedings. This approach stressed communally achieved unity and mitigated against the emergence of charismatic leadership, and even Fox faced some challenges to his pre-eminence in the Society. Among the most contentious issues was whether women's and men's meeting for workshop should be held separately or together. Theological disputes were of secondary importance, as the doctrine of the Inner Light meant that doctrinal purity was less important than ethical behaviour.

Fox and others took the faith overseas, both to Europe – notably the Netherlands and Germany – and across the Atlantic. Quakers were not welcome in the Puritan colonies of North America such as Massachusetts; Mary Dyer and three other Friends were hanged in Boston in 1660 (but Mary Fisher, another Quaker missionary to Boston, was expelled and went on a mission to convert the Ottoman sultan, whom she met in Adrianople).

Quakerism also flourished in the English colonies of Maryland, Rhode Island and Barbados; in 1681 Charles II made William Penn a gift of thousands of square miles of virgin territory. He named it Pennsylvania (after his father), and set about his 'Holy Experiment', attracting Quaker and sympathetic immigrants with a written constitution which offered free elections, trial by jury and toleration for all those who believed in any god – a constitution whose principles ultimately inspired the drafters of the Constitution of the United States itself. His laws against debauchery and 'idle amusements' were notably less stringent than those of the other religious colonies of that time. He also – unusually for his day – treated the Native Americans with evident respect and fairness.

While Pennsylvania began to flourish, in the mid-1680s the religious environment in England changed dramatically. The accession of James II brought to the throne a Catholic who sought to institute religious toleration as a step towards recognition of his own Catholic faith. Some 1,500 Quakers

An early meeting at Gracechurch Street, London, with the men and women on separate sides of the room.

Two of the most notable couples of the early days of the Quakers – William and Gulielma Penn and Gulielma's mother Mary and her husband Isaac Pennington – are commemorated with small plain gravestones at Jordans, Buckinghamshire.

were released from gaol, and some sided with the new king. He was, though, driven from the country in 1688 in the 'Glorious Revolution', an episode that was sealed with the Act of Toleration of 1689, which definitively ended the persecution of Quakers in England and allowed them to meet freely.

The years of persecution had forged the faith, but changed it too – no longer did Quakers believe, preach or act as if the Second Coming were imminent and that they alone were the true saints. Instead, they had come to focus on living ethically, maintaining their distinctive witness and waiting faithfully for the Last Days, whenever they would be. It was an approach that brought a very different style in the next century.

Mary Dyer, a Boston woman who had been converted to Quakerism on a trip to England in 1650, being led to the gallows in Boston in 1660.

19

A PECULIAR PEOPLE

IN THE AFTERMATH of the Act of Toleration of 1689, Quakers were free to pursue their faith, but many areas of public life remained closed to them in England – the professions, the universities and Parliament all required swearing oaths of loyalty, or acceptance of the Thirty-Nine Articles (adherence to the Church of England), which Friends – who argued that insisting on swearing an oath implied that a lower standard of truth must apply the rest of the time – consistently refused to do.

Rather than still seeing themselves as saints, they now described themselves as 'a peculiar people'. Where once they had been missionary, travelling and preaching to convert unbelievers, now they drew away from 'the World' (as they called the rest of society), holding themselves apart and living by their own rules.

A sombre dress code – undecorated grey coats and broad-brimmed hats for the men, plain grey dresses and white headdresses for the women – meant that they stood out from the fashionably colourful, bewigged world of the early eighteenth century. Their 'plain speech', with its distinctive use of 'thee' and 'thou', and their refusal to call the days of the week or months of the year by names that recalled pagan gods, also set them apart (Sunday 8 August was known to Quakers as First-day, the eighth day of the eighth month). They lived plainly too, abhorring music, painting and any form of artificial stimulation or entertainment as a worldly or sensual distraction from the Inner Light.

In 1738 London Yearly Meeting issued their first (handwritten) *Book of Discipline*, which collected advices that had been sent out to meetings over the previous decades and rules for the 'right ordering' of the Society. It was printed in 1783 and has remained the basis for Quaker faith and practice ever since. Also from this period date many of the Meeting Houses in cities, towns and villages across the country – plain houses, sometimes in austere classical style, studiously eschewing any religious symbolism or sense of sanctity or being set apart from the rest of God's creation.

Opposite: The Meeting House in Easton, Maryland, dating back to the 1680s. George Fox had visited the colony in the early 1670s.

A mixed Meeting in the eighteenth century.

A typical Quaker family at this time was highly patriarchal. Children were commonly disowned for 'marrying out' of the Society (on the grounds that they must have attended a church service). As a result, most Quakers were 'birthright' members of the Society, rather than what were known as 'Quakers by convincement' (converts); and the numbers in membership declined sharply.

Quaker dynasties emerged, and Quakers made little attempt to express their faith in terms that would influence the rest of society, focusing instead on the purity of their own lives. This was known as 'Quietism' – and it was manifested even in Quaker worship, with an increasing emphasis on waiting in silence, rather than on the vocal ministry that had been common in the previous century.

Even if the eighteenth century was relatively stagnant spiritually in the Society of Friends, the period saw two intellectual tendencies that were to have a profound, though conflicting, influence on the Society. The first was the rise of rationalism and scientific enquiry – the Quakers produced several important scientists during this period. The second was rise of Methodism, which began as a movement of renewal within the Church of England and proved to be a

The Meeting House in Flushing, New York, was built in the 1690s and is reputed to be the oldest house of worship in the state of New York.

Twenty-first century Quakers dressed in traditional eighteenth-century Quaker costume.

harbinger of a more widespread uprush of evangelical Christianity. By the early nineteenth century the Society had responded: an evangelical Quakerism emerged, which began to emphasise the importance of energetic engagement with society's ills. Thus Elizabeth Fry – who had been brought up in the Quietist tradition – took on the cause of prison reform, while others were deeply involved in the society to abolish the slave trade. They and other Evangelicals encouraged the gradual abandonment of the 'peculiarities' of the Quietist Quakers and brought in a new cohort of desperately needed converts.

An early-nineteenth-century painting of Quakers meeting for worship.

23

The enduring Quaker belief that the faith should be lived through social action stems from this period, and the evangelical strand of Quakerism, though now virtually extinct in Britain, flourished in the Americas, where it still survives. American Quakers never attempted to achieve a unity of organisation, as autonomous Yearly Meetings were mostly confined to a single state, and they deferred less and less to London. In the nineteenth century they showed a painful tendency to split. There were several faultlines, notably between those who maintained a belief in the literal truth of the Bible as the word of God; those who were prepared to take an enquiring, rational approach to the Christian message; and those who put all their trust in the 'Inner Light', even to the extent of moving away from Christianity and towards a more generalised deism.

In 1827–8, a major split – known as the Great Separation – occurred, beginning in Philadelphia and New York. Elias Hicks, a preacher from Long Island, New York, had won many followers, especially among the rural Quakers. He stressed 'obedience to the light within', downplaying study,

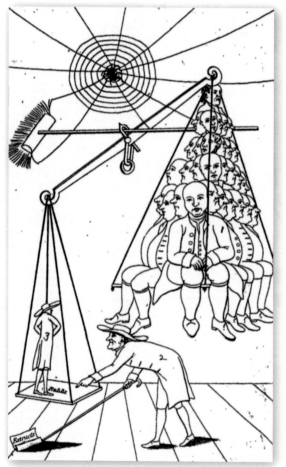

Below: A cartoon of 1828 showing the clerk of Philadelphia Yearly Meeting favouring a minority view, an act that led to the Great Separation.

Below right: Porcelain statue of Joseph John Gurney, the Norwich-born banker who travelled to the United States, where his views on the Inner Light caused a long-lasting schism in American Quakerism.

teaching and creedal tests and the authority of preachers of elders, and instead emphasising that the truth could be reached only through waiting for divine inspiration. In contrast, the more evangelical Orthodox Quakers – many of the urban and relatively sophisticated – emphasised scripture and insisted on the literal truth of Christianity. Several Yearly Meetings now suffered a destructive split that endured for many decades.

Further splits ensued twenty-five years later, among the Orthodox Yearly Meetings in New York and Ohio, when the traditionalist 'Conservative' followers of John Wilbur were disowned by the followers of English evangelical John Gurney, who preached that the Inner Light allowed the correct reading of the Bible. Further divisions continued to haunt American Quakers through the nineteenth century, until in 1902 attempts were made to bring together some of the divided Orthodox Yearly Meetings into a Friends United Meeting. The 1827 Separation finally ended in 1955, when the Yearly Meetings of New York, Canada and Philadelphia reunited.

In Britain, and in some parts of America, the end of the nineteenth century saw a decisive turn away from Gurneyite evangelical, mission-based Quakerism, as John Wilhelm Rowntree and New Englander Rufus Jones developed a full-blown liberal Quakerism, based on biblical scholarship and enquiry – even at the risk of abandoning the Christian roots of the faith. This period also saw the full entry of Quakers into civic life in Britain, where the restrictions on Quakers entering politics and the professions had been removed in 1870, while many of the 'peculiarities' – plain dress and speech, the rejection of gravestones, and so on – were finally dying out.

The evangelical-inspired missionary activity – which in the nineteenth century had mainly been directed towards the

Philadelphia City Hall, built in the 1880s and the world's highest building at the time, is topped with an 11-metre statue of Pennsylvania's founder William Penn.

Below left:
Rufus Jones,
the American
Quaker who
was influential in
revitalising liberal
Quakerism in
Britain at the
turn of the
twentieth century.

Below right:
Friends were
often active in
the Temperance
movement in
Britain before the
First World War.
While many
Quakers have
relaxed their
attitudes to
alcohol, they
remain strongly
opposed to
gambling.

poor and deprived parts of British cities – now moved overseas, to India, China and especially to East Africa and South America. Today, Quakers living in the latter two of these areas account for the majority of the world's Quakers, with Kenya alone having almost ten times as many Quakers as Britain by the year 2000.

In Britain, however, the Society, now overtly modernist in approach and urging its members to be 'open to new light, from whatever source it may come', became increasingly uncomfortable with Christian language, which began to feel exclusive of other truths. Yet, despite relatively small numbers (there have never been many more than about 25,000 people in membership, although many non-members frequently also attend Meetings and may play an active part in the life of the Society), it remained influential throughout the twentieth century, with Quakers maintaining a high-profile – and often deeply unpopular – pacifist stance during the two world wars, developing their pacifist position by working to build international institutions to prevent war, including the American Friends Service Committee and the United Nations, and working with influential charities to protect human rights and relieve suffering, including the Oxford Committee on Famine Relief (later Oxfam). From the 1960s, Quakers were also prominent in the Campaign for Nuclear Disarmament (CND) and associated organisations – and the Society itself found many new recruits from these movements.

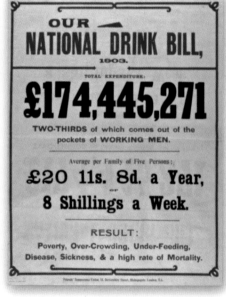

OUR ➤
NATIONAL DRINK BILL,
1903.

TOTAL EXPENDITURE:

£174,445,271

TWO-THIRDS of which comes out of the pockets of **WORKING MEN.**

Average per Family of Five Persons:

£20 11s. 8d. a Year,
or

8 Shillings a Week.

RESULT:
Poverty, Over-Crowding, Under-Feeding,
Disease, Sickness, & a high rate of Mortality.

By the beginning of the twenty-first century, the liberal Quakers of Britain Yearly Meeting – which has been characterised as adhering to the 'absolute perhaps' rather than any conventional creed – were a small fraction of the 350,000 Quakers worldwide. In the United States the full gamut of Quaker traditions still flourishes, while Evangelicals are found in many Third World countries. The different branches worship in different manners, with the liberal and conservative stressing 'unprogrammed' meetings, where worshippers wait in silence for inspiration to give ministry, while more evangelical Quaker meetings are led by pastors, with prayers, songs and preaching, interspersed by much shorter periods of silence.

Without any world-governing body that can struggle to reconcile these differences, the various traditions instead maintain friendly relations among those members who are interested. All tendencies look back to the insights of George Fox and the early Quakers, and mutual tolerance and goodwill remains high; unlike some other churches, even where substantial disagreement exists on such matters as sexual morality, few attempts are made to convince others of the wrongness of their beliefs. Among the 'advices and queries' that are regularly read at Meetings for Worship across Britain is the injunction 'think it possible you might be mistaken'. In an age of growing religious intolerance this marks out Quakers as remaining 'a peculiar people' – though in a quite new manner, suitable for the changing times.

A wedding from the early twentieth century after the Quakers had abandoned plain dress. The vows are kept simple, and the Meeting for Worship allows all guests to celebrate the couple.

THE PEACE TESTIMONY

W HATEVER THEIR DIFFERENCES, Quakers are known and respected for one essential part of their witness: their commitment to pacifism. Putting into practice the teachings of Jesus more literally than many other churches, Quakers have frequently placed themselves in great personal danger to bear witness to the essential wrongness of war, and many have extended this idea to a radical non-violence on a wide range of issues.

George Fox was not always a pacifist and sought converts among the Parliamentary army in the earliest years. In 1651, though, he also said:

> I told [the Commonwealth Commissioners] I lived in the virtue of that life and power that took away the occasion of all wars and I knew from whence all wars did rise, from lust ... I am come into the covenant of peace which was before wars and strifes were.

The peace testimony itself was the product of the early months of the Restoration era, when a group of religious radicals known as the Fifth Monarchy Men sought to instigate an uprising in London. Fearing that the Quakers would suffer in the inevitable backlash, Fox sought to distance his movement from the rebels by issuing a statement that has become a rallying cry for the Society:

> All bloody principles and practices we do utterly deny, with all outward wars, and strife, and fightings with outward weapons, for any end, or under any pretence whatsoever, and this is our testimony to the whole world. That spirit of Christ by which we are guided is not changeable, so as once to command us from a thing as evil and again to move unto it; and we do certainly know, and so testify to the world, that the spirit of Christ, which leads us into all Truth, will never move us to fight and war against any man with outward weapons, neither for the kingdom of Christ, nor for the kingdoms of this world.

Opposite: William Penn's treaty of 1682 with the Delaware Indians at Shackamaxon was celebrated by Quaker painter Benjamin West in 1771, and became widely known through prints and engravings.

A precursor of the peace testimony, issued by George Fox in advance of the Restoration of the monarchy in 1660.

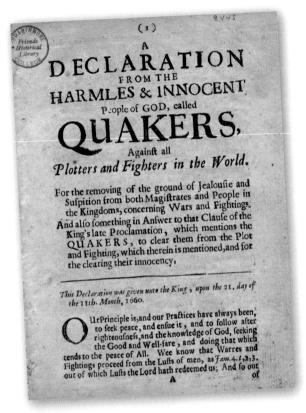

Bottom: Oxford Quakers bear witness to their peace testimony on Remembrance Day, 2011.

In the early years some of the most striking manifestations of the peace testimony came in the New World, where many settler communities were daily threatened by American Indians. But the Quaker colonies – East Jersey and Pennsylvania – refused to raise militias to defend themselves against either Native American or French attack. Instead, they set out to love their enemies. Thus, in Pennsylvania, William Penn agreed a famous treaty at Shackamaxon with the Delaware Indians, buying land from them at a fair price and exchanging wampum belts, asserting:

> We meet on the broad pathway of good faith and good-will; no advantage shall be taken on either side, but all shall be openness and love. We are the same as if one man's body was to be divided into two parts; we are of one flesh and one blood.

In the mid-eighteenth century the French writer Voltaire commented that this was the only treaty ever made between white men and the Indians that was never sworn to and never broken. (However, he spoke too soon: in 1763 a group of settlers known as the Paxton Boys killed twenty descendants of Indians who had lived peacefully since the 1690s on land donated by William Penn. The Pennsylvania frontier descended into anarchy.)

Penn was not the only Quaker to treat the Native Americans with respect. A famous incident occurred on the frontier in New York in 1775. In Easton, a village that was under regular attack, a group of armed Indians broke into the Meeting House as all the villagers sat in silent worship. The preacher Robert Nisbet urged all present to maintain their testimony by sitting in silence,

Robert Nisbet and Fierce Feathers, the American Indian chief moved by Quaker conviction and truth, in 1775.

until one by one, the armed men laid their weapons on the ground and sat at peace with the Friends. At the end of the Meeting, the chief said:

> We come to kill white man. See white men all sit quiet: no gun, no arrow, no knife; all quiet, all still, worshipping Great Spirit. Great Spirit is Indian, too. Then Great Spirit say to Indian: 'You must not kill these white men.'

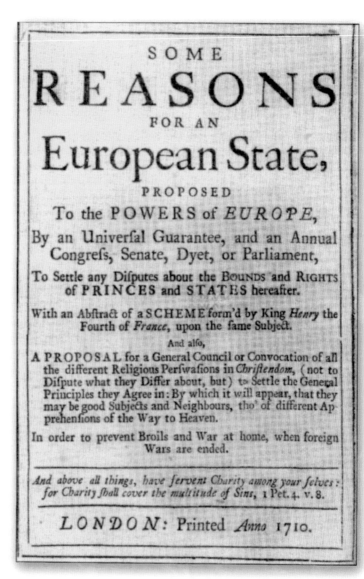

SOME

REASONS

FOR AN

European State,

PROPOSED

To the POWERS of *EUROPE*,

By an Univerſal Guarantee, and an Annual Congreſs, Senate, Dyet, or Parliament,

To Settle any Diſputes about the BOUNDS and RIGHTS of PRINCES and STATES hereafter.

With an Abſtract of a SCHEME form'd by King *Henry* the Fourth of *France*, upon the ſame Subject.

And alſo,

A PROPOSAL for a General Council or Convocation of all the different Religious Perſwaſions in *Chriſtendom*, (not to Diſpute what they Differ about, but) to Settle the General Principles they Agree in: By which it will appear, that they may be good Subjects and Neighbours, tho' of different Apprehenſions of the Way to Heaven.

In order to prevent Broils and War at home, when foreign Wars are ended.

And above all things, have fervent Charity among your ſelves: for Charity ſhall cover the multitude of Sins, 1 Pet. 4. v. 8.

LONDON: Printed *Anno* 1710.

One of several early proposals for an international body to resolve disputes and promote peace. Quakers have continued to believe in the value of internationalism.

He gave the Friends a white feather and an arrow as signs of peace, to display from their rooftop. There was no more war between them.

When caught up in conflict, Quakers have generally attempted to maintain their pacific testimony by being open to all, taking no sides and helping those who need assistance – a stance that has often been attacked as treacherous or cowardly. In the American War of Independence, many Quakers refused to fight and adopted a stance of strict neutrality, though others fought and some of them were disowned by the Society.

Quakers became engaged with relief work during the Franco-Prussian War of 1870–1. The star graphic, used as a badge by Quaker relief workers, became the symbol of the American Friends Service Committee in 1917.

In Ireland, when a violent revolt against British rule broke out in 1798, Abraham Shackleton of Ballitore, County Kildare, embodied the Quaker spirit by risking his life, making his home a place of sanctuary and feeding all those who needed 'sustenance'. Fifty years later, during the devastating Famine, Irish Quakers led the attempts to alleviate suffering, establishing soup kitchens across the country.

More direct attempts to stop war comprised direct appeals to those about to enter into combat or efforts to establish international institutions to resolve conflict before violence broke out. Thus, as early as 1678, Robert Barclay had made efforts at mediation, writing to the ambassadors of the princes of Europe, urging them to give up their evil ways. In 1850 Joseph Sturge tried to bring peace between the warring Denmark and the duchies of Schleswig-Holstein, and, four years later, a group of Friends went to meet the Tsar in St Petersburg in a vain attempt to avert the Crimean War (they also went to Finland to support the inhabitants of a region bombarded by the Royal Navy).

In mid-century America Quakers were much involved in campaigning against slavery, but rejected the drift into war. After the outbreak of hostilities, some Quakers claimed conscientious objector status, some paid fines to avoid military service, while others enlisted into the Union army.

Quakers were prominent in keeping the United States out of the First World War until 1917; and after war was finally declared, they set up the American Friends Services Committee to offer relief for those caught up in the war zone. They stayed in Europe through the interwar years and the Second World War, working in Spain during the Civil War, and assisting Jews to escape from Germany. In 1947 the American Friends Services Committee was awarded the Nobel Prize for peace, and continued its work in Europe and across the world through the Cold War and into the twenty-first century.

In Britain during the First World War most Quakers claimed conscientious objector status and refused to fight – frequently suffering imprisonment and accusations of cowardice, until the Friends Ambulance Unit was established, putting many Quakers in extreme danger on the frontline. Nevertheless, perhaps a third of Quakers who were eligible for the draft went to fight – and a similar proportion again fought against Nazism in the Second World War.

An American
Friends Service
Committee
advertisement
for support of
its relief effort in
Germany in 1945.

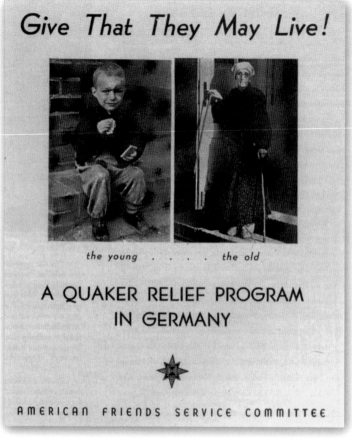

Give That They May Live!

the young . . . . the old

A QUAKER RELIEF PROGRAM IN GERMANY

AMERICAN FRIENDS SERVICE COMMITTEE

With the establishment of the League of Nations in 1919, Quakers set up an office in Geneva to work to avert interstate conflict. After the collapse of the League, it became involved in the creation of the United Nations and UNESCO, and has worked with them ever since for human rights, disarmament and global economic issues in an attempt to remove the causes of war. Quakers have continued to work to relieve distress and injustice, and to promote dialogue between communities in war zones across the world, including Palestine and Northern Ireland.

Many Quakers have extended their peace testimony by refusing to pay a proportion of their taxes that finances the military and by campaigning for disarmament. Already in the mid-eighteenth century, the Pennsylvanian Quaker John Woolman had urged the withholding a portion of taxes; and in the twentieth century, disarmament campaigns were powerful in the interwar years and especially so following the formation of the Campaign

Opposite:
The certificate
commemorating
the Nobel Prize
for Peace, awarded
to the American
Friends Service
Committee in
1947.

Det Norske Stortings Nobelkomite

har i Henhold til Reglerne i det af

ALFRED NOBEL

den 27de November 1895 oprettede Testamente tildelt

Friends Service Council

Nobels Fredspris for 1947

Oslo, 10de Desember 1947

Gunnar Jahn   Birger Braadland

Martin Tranmæl   Herman Smitt Ingebretsen

The real
tribulations of
life as a 'conshie'
(conscientious
objector) in the
First World War,
treated with
resilient humour
in this cartoon.

for Nuclear Disarmament in Britain in 1957. Quakers took a leading role in the disarmament movement, including at the Greenham Common women's camps in the 1980s and the campaigns against the Trident nuclear submarines in the 1990s and 2000s. They have been equally vocal in opposing Western military actions, for example, in Vietnam in the late 1960s, in the Balkans in the 1990s, in Iraq in 2003 and in Libya in 2011.

Some, inspired by Gandhi's message of non-violent resistance, undertook conscious campaigns of law-breaking to draw attention to what they saw as the greater criminality of preparing for nuclear war, for example, damaging military equipment symbolically to turn swords to ploughshares. Others have campaigned against the arms trade.

Left: Quakers protest in Washington against the Vietnam War in 1969.

Left Though one of the best-known Quakers, US President Richard Nixon is not perhaps the best advertisement for the Society.

Above: The Quaker protest about the Vietnam War had tragic consequences in 1969, when 31-year-old Norman Morrison set himself on fire in front of the Pentagon.

Although Quakers, faced with the horrors and moral crises of war, have always been challenged to find ways of living by the peace testimony, it has been, and remains, a crucial part of their witness to their faith. If Quakers are sure of anything, it is that 'war is not the answer' and that other ways must be found to resolve conflict. The testimony itself has developed new forms over the years, but trying to live up to George Fox's injunction that 'All bloody principles and practices we do utterly deny' remains the bedrock of being a Quaker.

Negro Slavery.

SPEECH

OF MR. HUTT,

To the Members of the Society of Friends, and the Friends of the Abolition of Slavery,

At the Kingston Hotel, on Thursday, September 6, 1832.

GENTLEMEN,

I THANK you very sincerely for the opportunity you have now afforded me of expressing to you the sentiments which I entertain on the subject of Colonial Slavery. I know that subject is so near the heart of every man who claims a philanthropic or christian character, that not merely in regard to the circumstances in which I now stand, but for my fair fame among those whose good opinion I am most anxious to cherish and deserve, I am extremely desirous that my sentiments upon it should be distinctly understood.

It is, I assure you, a great satisfaction to my own mind, that I can appear before you this day, and can state, in all sincerity of heart, that the opinions which I profess now are the same as I have always professed. No man can charge me, therefore, with having assumed these opinions for the promotion of any selfish or personal object. From the moment I went to the University to the hour I now stand before you, I have been, (and hundreds can bear testimony to the fact,) the zealous and ardent promoter of the Abolition of Slavery. *(Cheers.)*

The question appears to me now to have drawn itself into a very narrow compass, and to have assumed, I am happy to say, a very simple form; and I am sure, if the Friends of Humanity,—if the people of England, are only true to themselves, and to that great principle which carried the Act for the Abolition of the Slave Trade, I am perfectly satisfied that the extinction of Slavery might be effected at once and for ever.

With a view to explain what I mean, I will run over cursorily the heads of the history of the Slave Question. I believe it was in 1807, that that great act,—the first which was effected in the name of justice and humanity,—the Act for the Abolition of the Slave Trade,—passed the British Parliament. Lord Grenville, the Minister of the day, on laying it upon the table of the House of Lords, distinctly stated, that this measure was only to be regarded as a step to the final extinction of Slavery. It was not to be considered a final measure. It had reference to another measure, which was, the utter annihilation of Slavery. This view was adopted, in fact, and publicly declared, by most of the leading Members in both Houses of Parliament—by Mr. Sheridan, Mr. Canning, and others, as well as by Lord Grenville. This view of the question was likewise adopted by the Planters themselves. They said to Mr. Wilberforce and his Party, "Your object is now, in a great measure, accomplished; leave the rest to us; we will take care that your views shall be entirely carried into effect; but a gradual emancipation is necessary for the welfare of both parties; only give us time."—Mr. Wilberforce and the Friends of Humanity acquiesced in the proposition;—they thought they might cease from their labours, and that in the course of a short time they would have the satisfaction of knowing, that no man could live within the British Dominions and be a slave. Gentlemen, five and twenty years have now passed since that Act of Parliament was sanctioned by the Legislature;—during which time the Planter has been promising gradual emancipation. What then, you will ask, is now the condition of the slave? It is exactly what it was: at least, no amelioration has been effected by the voluntary act of the Planter. Some few measures have been adopted; but the Slave still continues a Slave, after five and twenty years have passed away! Yes, Gentlemen, in spite of the demands of justice,—in spite of the exertions of the Friends of Humanity,—in spite of the voice of twenty millions of people,—in spite of the authority of the British Parliament;—the system of Slavery still exists! Now, I ask, what is to be done? Will the Planters require five and twenty years more for the completion of this act of justice? Are we to delay, for half a century, the extinction of this atrocious and degrading system? I am sure you will not consent to it. I am sure we are not now to be told, that the slave owner is the best legislator for the slave; that the slave owner is the most proper guardian of his rights. *(Hear.)* I think it is now high time to come forward, and demand *the immediate Abolition of Slavery*. I know the Planter talks to us of his right in the slave, and of the rights of property. This language might have suited those times of bigotry and delusion which, thank heaven, have gone by for ever; but, in the present day such language is not an argument; it is an insult,—I will not stop to refute it. It has been refuted by far higher powers than mine. It is only necessary to notice it, in order that it may be despised.—*(Cheers.)* The planter says that insurrection and bloodshed will arise; that the slave is in a condition unfit for freedom; and that if we put freedom in his possession, it will prove a curse not merely to his master, but to himself—that he is a mean, wretched, sordid, degraded animal. Gentlemen, I know that he is so. How in the name of reason should he be otherwise! During the course of five and twenty years of gradual abolition, he has been surrounded by nothing but cruelty, oppression, and crime,—by slavery, and by that utter depravation of moral feeling of which slavery is alternately the cause and the consequence. I now demand,—I trust the people of England will demand,—of the slave-owner, the renunciation of his preposterous claims.—*(Hear.)* Some preparation may, indeed, be necessary, in order to fit the slave for the enjoyment of his freedom; but this I think is perfectly plain, that the slave-owner either cannot or will not adopt the measures necessary for that purpose. I think five and twenty years' experience is sufficient to satisfy us, that this preparation must no longer be entrusted to his hands.—*(Hear.)* Gentlemen, I think we should take it out of his hands. I would require of him at once that the slave should be free. He tells us, that a scene of bloodshed and insurrection must ensue. Most unquestionably, it is the duty of every wise and humane man to take every proper precaution that the measure which rescues the Negro from Slavery shall not involve society in bloodshed or confusion. Still, I would commence with saying, "The Slave shall be free." *(Hear.)* I would put under the controul,—not of the Planter, but of the Parliament,—the then situation of the Slave. I would allow other men, who, recognizing the Negro no longer as a bondman, would undertake that duty, to promote, as much as possible, his social, moral, and religious character, to prepare him for enjoying the blessings of liberty, which is equally the right of the black man and the white,—the indefeasable right of every human being upon earth. *(Cheers.)*

This, then, Gentlemen, is my argument:—The extinction of Slavery, has been, for many years past, the object before us. The extinction of Slavery by the intervention of the Planters, and a gradual process, has been put to the test of a fair and adequate experiment. What has been the consequence? It has failed,—cruelly and entirely failed. *(Hear.)* It is clear we must adopt another system; and that system I would commence, by declaring, in the outset,—the Negro is free. *(Cheers.)* Having established that principle, I might think it necessary to place him under the restraint of persons who would undertake the care of his education. But I look upon it as an object of first-rate importance, to establish the principle immediately,—that man can no longer hold property in man. *(Applause.)*

I will not go into the question of the rights of property,—the right which the slave-owner presumes to set up in the blood and muscles of his fellow creature. That question has been settled by higher powers and far happier quarters. Nor will I go into the question, (for that too has been settled) how far we should neglect our duty, because the Colonial Assemblies have neglected theirs. I have stated to you, simply and plainly, the views I entertain on the question of West India Slavery. Whether it may be my lot to advocate these views in a public character, as your Representative, or in what would be to me, in many respects, the more enviable situation of private and domestic life, I assure you this question will always command the best energies which it is in my humble power to afford.— *(Applause.)*

I have now, Gentlemen, only to thank you for your great kindness in coming here, and for the attention you have paid me. I hope the explanation I have given will appear satisfactory. With respect to any other matters, involved in the choice of a Representative, I will only say, I shall be extremely happy to answer any questions which any Gentleman may think proper to put to me. I have nothing to conceal, and am most anxious to give every explanation with respect to my views and conduct, that any Gentleman can require.

THAT OF GOD IN EVERYONE

FOR GEORGE FOX, Quakerism was never simply a question of waiting in silence. It was and still is an active, practical faith that has brought many of its adherents to the forefront of movements for reform and social justice. In this it is based on the belief in absolute equality of all.

The first radical effect of this belief was the notion that women were the equals of men and could minister on the same basis as men. Even a century after the foundation of the Society, a traditional Englishman like Samuel Johnson could still be surprised by this aspect of the Society; he commented, 'A woman's preaching is like a dog walking on his hind legs. It is not done well; but you are surprised to find it done at all.' In practice, this equality was not complete throughout the Society, as in some Meeting Houses women were separated from men by a screen, women were excluded from the administrative Meeting for Sufferings, and in Britain a separate range of Women's Meetings existed at every level up to Yearly Meeting until the twentieth century.

But women's rights have formed an important part of the Quaker message. In the mid-nineteenth century the American Friend Lucretia Mott organised the 1848 Seneca Falls Convention on Women's Rights, which began the movement for women's suffrage in the United States. Quakers such as Alice Paul remained integral to the women's movement in the United States, more perhaps than in Britain, but on both sides of the Atlantic women's rights have been a key Quaker concern, and many Quakers work with disadvantaged women across the world. In 1946 the American Emily Greene Balch shared the Nobel Peace Prize for her work with the Women's International League for Peace and Freedom (WILPF), a movement of and for women, campaigning for peace.

An aspect of human affairs related to gender is sexuality, and Quakers have again been at the forefront of the recognition of gay relationships. In 1964, when homosexuality was still illegal, a group of British Friends published

Opposite: Quaker opposition to slavery was increasingly vocal on both sides of the Atlantic in the first half of the nineteenth century. This speech was given shortly before slavery was abolished in British Colonies.

Right: Lucretia Mott, a travelling minister from Massachusetts, campaigned ceaselessly against slavery and for women's rights in the decades before the Civil War.

Far right: Levi Coffin was nicknamed 'President of the Underground Railroad' for helping thousands of slaves to escape via Indiana and Ohio to the north.

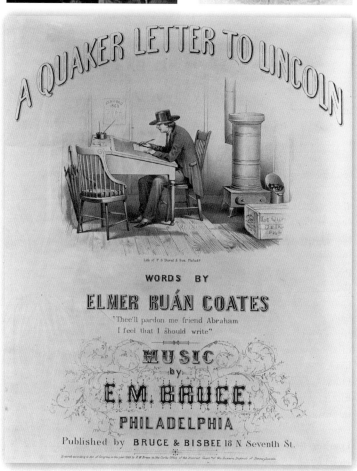

The song-sheet for an anti-slavery song of the 1860s.

Towards a Quaker View of Sex, which emphasised that loving, non-exploitative relationships should be supported, whatever the gender of the couple. In recent years liberal Quakers in Britain and elsewhere have actively supported the move towards same-sex marriage. By no means all Quakers support this approach, and many individual Meetings take their own line on this subject, with many Conservative Friends in the United States, and many Evangelicals in many other countries, opposing it in favour of a strict reading of the Bible.

The contribution of Quakers to the anti-slavery cause has already been mentioned, and members of the Society formed the vast majority of the active members of the Society for Effecting the Abolition of the Slave Trade, which campaigned in the decades leading up to the decisive legislation in 1807. In the United States Quakers (including Thomas Paine) campaigned unsuccessfully against slavery before and in the aftermath of the War of Independence and urged individual slave-owners to free their slaves. In the 1850s and 1860s Quakers played an active part in the establishment of the 'Underground Railroad' that assisted fugitive slaves to escape from the south to Canada: one Quaker, Levi Coffin, a trader operating in Indiana and Ohio, personally aided 2,000 ex-slaves.

Humane care of the mentally ill is another field in which Quakers made the running, notably with the foundation of The Retreat, a hospital opened in York by William Tuke in 1796, at which time the typical 'lunatic asylum' offered little more than imprisonment, torture and public humiliation. Tuke saw inmates as potentially rational beings: he let them wear their own clothing and encouraged them to engage in handicrafts and to study.

Society's mistreatment of inmates of another institution, the prison, has been another long-running Quaker concern. This began when Elizabeth Fry, a member of the influential Gurney banking family, was taken by a friend to visit London's Newgate prison in 1813. Horrified by the overcrowding (more

American Quakers stepped up their ministry against slavery in the decades leading up to the Civil War.

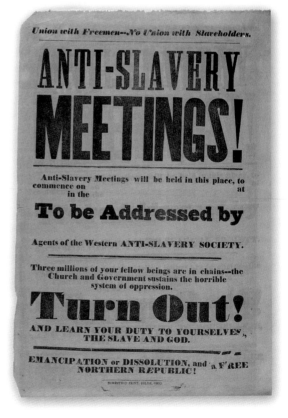

Elizabeth Fry
prepares to visit
the female inmates
of Newgate prison.

Above: A mug celebrating William Wilberforce and the anti-slavery message from the late eighteenth century.

Below: A Quaker vigil in 2008 against the unjust treatment of Australian aboriginals.

than thirty women – many awaiting trial – and children to a cell), she began visiting the prison and then established a national women's campaign (the first of its kind), calling for reform. She urged that 'punishment is not for revenge, but to lessen crime and reform the criminal', and she continued to work in prisons with the poor and the sick until her death in 1845.

Other Quakers have worked to alleviate poverty. Seebohm Rowntree, son of Joseph the industrialist and philanthropist, made three pioneering studies of poverty in York, arguing in the first of these in 1899 that poverty was the result of low wages rather than fecklessness or even unemployment. In later life he worked with William Beveridge, influencing the development of the British Welfare State. In the twentieth century many Quakers responded to concerns about poverty by working for economic justice in the Third World, educating, improving living conditions and assisting people in combating the dominance of First World corporations.

THE INNER LIGHT

Alongside the peace testimony, the doctrine of the Inward Light (or Inner Light, though this term was rarely used until the twentieth century) is what makes Quakerism distinctive. George Fox described it in his Journal of 1648:

> Every man was enlightened by the divine light of Christ; and I saw it shine through all, and they that believed it came out of condemnation and into the light of life and became the children of it … This I saw in the pure openings of the Light without the help of any man, neither did I then know where to find it in the Scriptures; though afterwards, searching the Scriptures, I found it.

This understanding lies at the heart of what makes Quakers so individual; so personally responsible for their own moral choices and behaviour. Quakers are given two related pieces of advice: 'Bring the whole of your life under the ordering of the spirit of Christ'; and also, 'Let your life speak'. In this chapter we look in a little more detail at three Quakers who lived at very different times but whose lives and works spoke loudly of their understanding of the Inner Light. Between them, they exemplify some of the many perennial concerns of Quakers, including gender equality, principled opposition to slavery and economic exploitation, and the need to work internationally through political channels for peace.

MARGARET FELL (1614–1702)

Often called the 'mother of Quakerism', Margaret Fell was born into the Lancashire gentry and was wife of Judge Thomas Fell MP of Swarthmoor Hall and mother of nine children. In June 1652 George Fox visited and made a deep impression on her when he said that there was no value in repeating the teachings of others, however eminent, unless the truth comes from the heart ('You will say, "Christ saith this, and the apostles say this"; but what canst thou say? Art thou a child of Light, and hast thou walked in the Light, and what thou speakest, is it inwardly from God?'). These words drew her irresistibly to stand up in her pew: 'This opened me so that it cut me to the heart; and then I saw clearly we were all wrong. So I sat down in my pew again and cried bitterly.' She left the Anglican Church and persuaded her husband to support, if not actually to join, the nascent Quaker movement.

Thomas Fell permitted his house to become Fox's unofficial headquarters and Margaret set up a fund to support travelling Quaker ministers and to assist them when they fell into trouble with the law. Her husband's death in 1658 left her a wealthy widow, and she herself began to travel to spread the word and to broaden her role in the movement. She regularly wrote to Oliver Cromwell and both corresponded with and spoke directly to Charles II on behalf of the Quakers. She was arrested and imprisoned in Lancaster Castle for more than four years for allowing illegal Quaker meetings to be held at Swarthmoor and refusing to swear the Oath of Allegiance to the king. Her defence was simple: 'as long as the Lord blesses me with a home, I shall worship him in it.'

While in prison, she published *Women's Speaking Justified*, a groundbreaking book on the right of women to minister, and she was the moving force behind

Swarthmoor Hall, Margaret Fell's home, became the centre of the early Quaker movement and is still the destination of Quaker pilgrimages.

the revolutionary notion of separate women's meetings, which began in the 1650s. With the addition of separate women's business meetings for overseeing the members and caring for the sick and the poor, she gradually won the support of Fox. Her reputation among Quakers grew the longer she stayed in prison, and after her release, she and George Fox married in October 1669. Fox's peripatetic ministry, plus further spells in prison for each, meant they spent little time together, other than a year at Swarthmoor in 1675–6.

Margaret continued to make Swarthmoor the general Quaker base and corresponded widely within the movement, and in the 1670s she was the leading light of the Swarthmoor Women's Monthly Meeting, during which she took a key role in defining and modelling the life of a Quaker woman. Her views on the important role of women within the life of the Society as a whole sometimes caused controversy and resentment; in particular her ideas concerning the Women's Meeting's role in approving marriages.

She continued her leading role in the Society, writing regular epistles to meetings across the country, and maintained her activism, even after Fox's death in 1691. In 1700, just a year before her own death aged eighty-eight, she was advising Quakers not to follow the 'silly poor gospel' of plain dress.

A Meeting of solemn Quakers in the late seventeenth century, listening to the word of God preached by a woman.

Throughout her long and formative commitment to the faith, she suffered many personal deprivations, yet shaped the young Society and carved out a radical and highly influential path so that women could take part in the public realm.

CONSIDERATIONS
ON KEEPING
NEGROES;
Recommended to the PROFESSORS of
CHRISTIANITY, of every *Denomination.*

PART SECOND.

By *JOHN WOOLMAN.*

Ye shall not respect Persons in Judgment; but you shall hear the Small as well as the Great: You shall not be afraid of the Face of Man; for the Judgment is GOD's. Deut. i. 17.

JOHN WOOLMAN (1720–72)

John Woolman was the archetype of the campaigning Quaker, driven by the testimonies to fight for justice and to urge fundamental changes in the way people lived. Born to a Quaker family in New Jersey and a tailor by trade, John Woolman's life changed when, aged twenty-three, he was told by his employer to write a bill of sale for a female black slave. Some time later he was asked to write a will for a Friend, which included disposing of a slave; when he protested that buying and selling other humans was a sin against the Light, he persuaded the man to set the slave free.

At this time, few Friends were concerned by slavery – even though George Fox had spoken about

As well as trying to be faithful to the testimonies of equality and peace, Woolman powerfully pursued the testimony of simplicity, refusing to use silver or gold utensils, or to wear dyed clothes – because of the hardships and dangers endured by those engaged in the manufacture of such objects. This meant he dressed in an unusual manner, with a white hat, linen shirt, white stockings and shoes of uncured leather. He lived respectfully with the Indians (seeing that for them, as for the black people, 'the seeds of great calamity and desolation are sown and growing fast on this continent'), refused to pay the portion of his taxes that paid for war, and campaigned for the poor and for animal welfare, preferring to walk rather than ride in carriages.

In 1772 he travelled to England, insisting on travelling steerage in sympathy with the enslaved Africans. He visited London Yearly Meeting, where his appearance shocked many, but he powerfully and effectively urged the Society to oppose slavery. A few months later, he died in York. His journal of the years 1756–70 has been read by Quakers and many others ever since.

Philip Noel-Baker (see overleaf) was a key figure in the establishment of the Friends Ambulance Unit in 1914, allowing Quaker conscientious objectors to offer their assistance to those suffering horribly on the Western Front. As the damage to this vehicle shows, the ambulance men placed themselves in great danger in the course of their duties.

PHILIP NOEL-BAKER (1889–1982)

Politician, diplomat, Olympic athlete and peace campaigner, Noel-Baker is the only individual Quaker to have won the Nobel Prize for Peace (and the only person to combine a Nobel Prize with an Olympic medal). His father, also a Quaker, had been a progressive MP. During the First World War, Philip, a conscientious objector, organised the Friends Ambulance Unit and served in France and Italy, being awarded several medals for valour.

An internationalist, after the War, he attended the Paris Peace Conference and was involved in the establishment of the League of Nations, before entering Parliament in 1924 as a Labour MP. In the 1930s he worked consistently

Philip Noel-Baker in 1942, when he was the Minister for War Transport. After the war he held several ministerial posts, and was chairman of the Labour Party, 1946–7.

for disarmament and collective security. He served as a minister during the Second World War and during the Attlee government, organising the London Olympic Games in 1948. He continued to support the Olympic movement throughout his long life, saying, 'In a nuclear age, sport is man's best hope.'

He was in charge of British preparatory work for the United Nations from 1944, helped to draft the UN Charter at San Francisco in 1945 and in 1946 was a member of the British delegation. He was thus deeply involved in the creation of both of the twentieth century's great experiments in international organisation, and in 1959 he was awarded the Nobel Peace Prize for his long commitment to multilateral nuclear disarmament.

The Quaker Tapestry celebrates the Friends Ambulance Unit and the help it has given to those needing medical help at times of war.

FRIENDS AMBULANCE UNIT 1914-19 1939-46 1946-59

A record of goodwill and positive service by conscientious objectors in twentyfive countries suffering as a result of war

TRADE, POLITICS, LEARNING AND THE ARTS

BOTH DURING the Quietist phase and thereafter, Quakers have shaped society in all kinds of ways, in both Britain and the Americas.

From the earliest days, George Fox and his associates regularly fell foul of the law, and though they frequently suffered at its hands, they came to understand it well and sometimes to use it to their advantage. But some, including William Penn and Margaret Fell, were well known at court and had the ear of Charles II. Penn later acted as an advisor to James II and encouraged his policy of religious toleration. Yet, as a Quaker prominent in national politics, he was – and remains – unusual.

In the mid-nineteenth century the first Quakers entered Parliament, and John Bright was a distinguished radical Member and famous orator. But politics, the art of the possible, is not always compatible with maintaining a purely spiritual witness: even Bright found himself deviating from the Quaker testimonies – he supported the suppression of the Indian War of Independence in 1857, for example. Since that time, Quakers within mainstream politics have tended to campaign for international institutions to foster peace. Many others, however, have preferred to campaign on issues rather than engage with party politics.

In the United States similar tensions occurred. Pennsylvania had deviated in large part from its Quaker principles by the mid-eighteenth century, and some Yearly Meetings (that of North Carolina, for example, in the 1850s) actively discouraged their members from engaging in seeking election at all. Dolley Madison, wife of the fourth president, was a Quaker but did not significantly influence her husband's policies. It is ironic and a little sad that the two Quakers to have held the supreme office, Herbert Hoover and Richard Nixon, are among the least admired of American presidents, though

Hoover's term in office, which was marred by the Wall Street Crash, has recently been convincingly rehabilitated. He remained within the faith in which he had been brought up, as did, perhaps surprisingly, Richard Nixon, who had been brought up in the conservative and evangelical Quaker tradition of California, and who held Quaker Meetings in the White House. When, during his presidency, liberal Quakers asked his Meeting to disown him for his military aggression and his lying to the public, they did not respond.

Rather than pursue politics, from the eighteenth century, Quakers frequently opted for three important routes to prosperity and influence – banking, industry and the sciences, and to each area they brought personal discipline, frugality and drive, harnessed by an increasingly prosperous and tight-knit network of connections within the Society, which allowed them to play a vital and positive part in the history of their country.

The insistence on plain speaking – which meant they refused to barter and prided themselves on keeping their word – quickly gained them the reputation of honest traders, and by the mid-eighteenth century, they put this to good use. Several – such as draper David Barclay in London, iron-master Sampson Lloyd in Birmingham, flax-dresser James Backhouse in Darlington,

Two great mid-nineteenth-century Quaker radicals, John Bright and Joseph Sturge, with their non-Quaker colleague Richard Cobden (right), 'finding peace', according to French caricaturist Honoré Daumier.

Right: Samuel Hoare, one of the many successful Quaker bankers of the eighteenth century. His bank eventually became part of Barclays.

Below: The Iron Bridge near Coalbrookdale, symbol of the technological revolution begun there by Abraham Darby in the early eighteenth century.

and wool merchants John and Henry Gurney in Norwich – had moved from their trades to banking, and the provincial businesses they established eventually evolved into the international Barclays Bank and Lloyds TSB.

The bankers were at the heart of strong networks among the Quaker traders and merchants, with each party supporting the other and guaranteeing commercial success over their rivals.

Quaker links with industry were equally important to the evolution of the Industrial Revolution. Abraham Darby, an active Friend based in Bristol, established an iron foundry at Coalbrookdale in Shropshire in 1709, where he developed a revolutionary technique of smelting or producing pig-iron in a blast furnace using coke. His son and grandson, both Abraham Darby, developed the business, the technology and the site, until by mid-century, it was a busy industrial centre, with potteries and tile factories as well as ironworks and factories for metal consumer goods. In 1780 the world's first bridge in cast iron opened over the nearby gorge.

The commercial and technical success of iron casting at Coalbrookdale was spread around the country via a new network of canals, and again Quakers were often instrumental in developing these. Thus, wool merchant John Hustler financed and masterminded the Leeds and Liverpool Canal and the Bradford Canal, on which that town's nineteenth-century prosperity was built. A few decades later, the Pease family, very wealthy Quaker wool merchants and colliery owners in county Durham, built the world's first steam railway from Stockton to Darlington, which opened in 1825 (seven years later, Joseph Pease became the first Quaker to be elected to Parliament).

The world's first passenger railway, opened in 1825 between Stockton and Darlington, was the brainchild of Quakers.

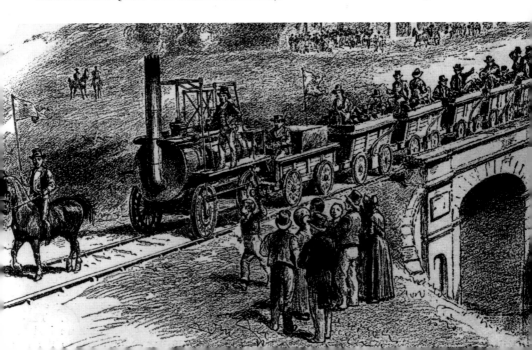

One British industry that was dominated by Quakers was confectionery; in particular cocoa and chocolate. The first to capture this market was the apothecary Joseph Fry, who set up his business in Bristol in 1753 and, by the end of the century, bequeathed a huge industry to his son, Joseph Storrs Fry, who promoted chocolate and cocoa as healthy, pure but inexpensive foodstuffs, before expanding into confectionery. Fry's main competitors were also Quakers, notably the Rowntree firm based in York and Cadbury's in Birmingham.

Both of these companies took their social responsibilities particularly seriously: Joseph Rowntree provided excellent welfare for his workers, while in 1893 George Cadbury created the model village of Bournville for the factory staff, giving the houses decent gardens, and providing parks, sports facilities, schools and so on. Shoe manufacturers C. & J. Clark launched a similar initiative in Street, Somerset.

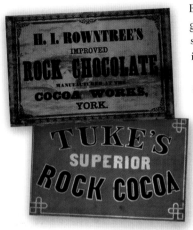

Science and technology were equally important areas of Quaker endeavour. Many of the great clockmakers of the late seventeenth and early eighteenth centuries were apparently Quakers, including Thomas Tompion, Daniel Quare and George Graham. The number of Quakers who have been allowed to join Britain's prestigious scientific society, the Royal Society, has been quite disproportionate compared with other members. They include John Dalton, whose atomic theory (1808) is the foundation for modern chemistry; Thomas Young,

The York-based Tuke family firm developed a successful chocolate business in the mid-nineteenth century, which was bought to form the basis of Rowntree's in 1862.

The Rest House in Bournville, near Birmingham – the model village built by George Cadbury for the workers in his nearby factory.

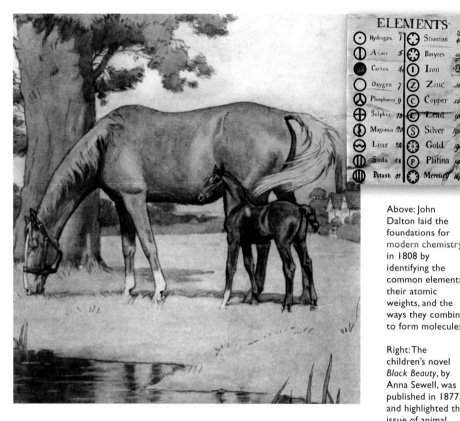

ELEMENTS·

☉	Hydrogen	1	✛ Strontian	46
①	Azote	5	✸ Barytes	68
●	Carbon	5	Ⓘ Iron	50
○	Oxygen	7	Ⓩ Zinc	56
⊗	Phosphorus	9	Ⓒ Copper	56
⊕	Sulphur	13	Ⓛ Lead	90
◐	Magnesia	20	Ⓢ Silver	190
⊖	Lime	24	⊛ Gold	190
⓪	Soda	28	Ⓟ Platina	190
Ⓜ	Potash	42	✸ Mercury	167

Above: John Dalton laid the foundations for modern chemistry in 1808 by identifying the common elements, their atomic weights, and the ways they combine to form molecules.

Right: The children's novel *Black Beauty*, by Anna Sewell, was published in 1877, and highlighted the issue of animal cruelty. This scence is from the start of the novel 'The first place that I can well remember was a large pleasant meadow with a pond of clear water in it.'

who demonstrated the wave theory of light; and surgeon Joseph Lister, who pioneered antiseptic surgery. Many Quakers have been astronomers, including Arthur Eddington, who has been called the father of modern astrophysics and who was the first to demonstrate experimentally the predictions of Einstein's general theory of relativity. The Quaker connection with astrophysics continued into the later twentieth century with Jocelyn Bell-Burnell, who played an important role in the discovery of pulsars in the 1960s.

American Quakers have been similarly prominent in science and technology, including the eighteenth-century Pennsylvanian botanist, John Bartram, and Baltimore railroad pioneer, Philip E. Thomas. However, they tended to be more prominent in the arts. Several of the greatest American writers of the nineteenth century, including Herman Melville, author of *Moby-Dick*, and poets Walt Whitman and Ralph Waldo Emerson, were all greatly influenced by Quakerism. Melville's novel includes many Quaker characters, while Whitman was brought up as a Quaker and displayed Quaker practices in his life without formally being a member of the Society.

American artist Edward Hicks painted more than sixty versions of *The Peaceable Kingdom*, based on Isaiah's vision of the lion lying down with the lamb.

He was greatly influenced by the Pennsylvanian Quaker artist Edward Hicks, notable for his series of paintings in naïve style of '*The Peaceable Kingdom*' and key scenes from Quaker history, including the painting of William Penn's Treaty with the Indians. Another notable American-born painter – though he pursued his career in London – was the history painter Benjamin West, who became president of the Royal Academy in 1792.

While eighteenth-century British Quakers had been suspicious of fiction, they encouraged journal writing, and many Quaker women in particular wrote fine examples. In the 1870s Anna Sewell, from Norfolk, wrote *Black Beauty*, the enduringly popular novel that influentially drew attention to cruelty to horses.

The twentieth century has seen a range of notable Quakers in the arts: the novelist James A. Michener was a Quaker; and actors Judi Dench, Paul Eddington, Ben Kingsley and Sheila Hancock have all been members of the Society, as was film star James Dean in the USA.

LIVE ADVENTUROUSLY

W HILE QUAKERS RARELY ACT without careful deliberation, they are not often cautious. One of the most quoted Quaker injunctions is 'live adventurously', and many seek to do just that. Silence may be valued highly, but Quietism is very much a thing of the distant past.

Advices and Queries also says, 'Try to discern new growing points in social and economic life. Seek to understand the causes of injustice, social unrest and fear.' This is taken very seriously. Quakers often put their lives on the line to do so – literally in the case of peace-workers who seek out the world's trouble spots, such as Iraq, where American Friend Tom Fox was taken hostage and killed in 2006.

Others seek to find new ways through equally challenging areas: in the early 2000s, a time in Britain of great fear and hostility towards sex offenders, Quakers led the way in creating 'circles of support and accountability' for offenders after their release from prison. They offered some rare human contact for people who were otherwise isolated if not ostracised, and discouraged repeat offending. Initial pilot projects were praised by police and other authorities, and the initiative was developed more widely. Restorative justice – whereby offenders are expected to take responsibility for what they have done and, where possible, directly to address the hurt done to the victim – has been another important Quaker initiative and is gradually reaching wider public awareness and acceptance.

Every Quaker meeting is a hive of initiatives to make

Some young Quakers in Bolivia. Quaker missionaries first came to Bolivia in 1919, and Bolivia now has the third-largest population of Quakers in the world.

the world, the local district, and the Meeting itself, a better place. Quakers take the lead on seeking new ways of breaking down social injustices, supporting food banks or building medical centres for homeless people. A sense of the overwhelming urgency of international justice leads many to get involved with a host of activities concerned with Third-World development, health or education, or economic initiatives, including fair-trade issues. Others whose concern focuses on environmental degradation and climate change take a lead on exploring an equally complex set of practical low-carbon ways of living. Issues – theoretical, political and practical – are debated continually, and Quakers are often among the first to sign up to demonstrations, letter-writing campaigns or leafleting the neighbourhood. Many actively supported the Occupy movement in 2011–12.

Quakers have taken an active part in the long protest against nuclear weapons; here they prepare to protest at the British nuclear submarine base at Faslane.

While churches of many denominations may see some or all of these activities, Quakers have proved able to win people's trust in an enormous

Quakers in Seattle 'baking for peace'.

range of circumstances. Their humanistic approach – stressing Christ's ministry rather than his divinity, reminding themselves to 'think it possible you may be mistaken' and rarely speaking of sin or falsehood, nor showing much concern for heaven or hell – is in stark and welcome contrast to the fundamentalism that has grown up in recent decades. Quakers are often deeply involved in initiatives to bring faiths of all kinds together and to break down mistrust and fear.

This diversity of activity reflects the diversity of the Quaker Church itself. The 'typical' Quakers of the Anglo-Saxon world are a small minority of Friends around the world – with four out of every five Quakers now to be found in evangelical Meetings in East Africa or South America.

In terms of numbers, liberal Quakerism – which had its last great injection of new blood in the anti-nuclear peace movements of the 1980s – may be on a gentle decline, absolutely as well as relatively; but it continues to throb with urgency and still performs a vital function, identifying and facing some of the most difficult issues that too many others ignore.

For all Quakers try to follow George Fox's injunction: 'Be patterns, be examples in all countries, places, islands, nations, wherever you go, so that your carriage and life may preach among all sorts of people, and to them. Then you will come to walk cheerfully over the world, answering that of God in every one.'

The world today desperately needs them.

The final panel from the Quaker Tapestry, celebrating the world family of Friends.

PLACES TO VISIT

Bunhill Fields Burial Ground, 38 City Road, London EC1Y 1AU.
Telephone: 020 7374 4127.
Friends House, 173 Euston Road, London NW1 2BJ.
Telephone: 020 7663 1094/1095. Website: www.friendshouse.co.uk
Ironbridge Gorge Museum, Coach Rd, Coalbrookdale, Shropshire TF8 7DQ.
Telephone: 01952 435900. Website: www.ironbridge.org.uk
Jordans Meeting House, Welders Lane, Jordans, Buckinghamshire HP9 2SN.
Telephone: 01494 876594. Website: www.quaker.org.uk/jordans
The Peace Museum, 10 Piece Hall Yard, Bradford, West Yorkshire BD1 1PJ.
Telephone: 01274 780241. Website: www.peacemuseum.org.uk
Peckover House and Garden, National Trust, North Brink, Wisbech PE13 1JR.
Telphone: 01945 583463. Website: www.nationaltrust.org.uk/peckover-house
The Quaker Tapestry Exhibition Centre, Friends Meeting House, Stramongate, Kendal,
Cumbria LA9 4BH. Telephone: 01539 722975. Website: www.quaker-tapestry.co.uk
Selly Manor Museum, Oak Tree Lane, Bournville, Birmingham B30 1UB.
Telephone: 0121 472 3831. Webstie: www.sellymanormuseum.org.uk
Swarthmoor Hall, Swarthmoor Hall Lane, Ulverston, Cumbria LA12 0JQ.
Telephone: 01229 583204. Website: www.swarthmoorhall.co.uk
Woodbrooke Quaker Study Centre, 1046 Bristol Road, Birmingham B29 6LJ.
Telephone: 0121 472 5171. Website: www.woodbrooke.org.uk

UNITED STATES
Flushing Quaker Meeting House, 137–16 Northern Boulevard, Flushing, New York 11354.
Telephone: 001 718 358 9636.
Friends Center, 1501 Cherry Street, Philadelphia PA 19102.
Telephone: 001 215 241 7000. Website: www.friendscentercorp.org
Herbert Hoover National Historic Site Information, 110 Parkside Drive West Branch,
Iowa IA 52358. Telephone: 001 319 643 2541. Website: www.nps.gov/heho
John Woolman Memorial, Mt Holly, 99 Branch Street, Mt Holly, New Jersey NJ 08060-
1866. Telephone: 001 609 267 3226.
Levi Coffin House, 113 U.S. 27 North, P.O. Box 77, Fountain City, Indiana IN 47341.
Telephone: 001 765 847 2432.
Pennsbury Manor, 400 Pennsbury Memorial Road, Morrisville, Pennsylvania PA 19067.
Telephone: 001 215 946 0400. Website: www.pennsburymanor.org

FURTHER READING

Advices and Queries. Britain Yearly Meeting, 1995.

Cadbury, Deborah. *Chocolate Wars*. Harper Press, 2008.

Durham, Geoffrey. *The Spirit of the Quakers*. Yale University Press, 2010.

Fox, George (edited by John Nicholls). *Journal of George Fox*. Cambridge University Press, 1962.

Gray, Simon. *Quaker Faith and Practice around the world*. Kindle edition, 2005.

Ingle, Larry. *First Among Friends: George Fox and the Creation of Quakerism*. Oxford University Press, 1994.

Moore, Rosemary. *The Light in the Consciences: The Early Quakers in Britain 1646–1666*. Pennsylvania State University Press, 2000.

Nicholls, Ann. *The Golden Age of Quaker Botanists*. Quaker Tapestry at Kendal, 2007.

A Pictorial Guide to the Quaker Tapestry. Quaker Tapestry at Kendal, 1992.

Pink Dandelion, Ben. *The Quakers: A Very Short Introduction*. Oxford University Press, 2010.

Punshon, John. *Portrait in Grey: A short history of the Quakers*. Britain yearly Meeting, 1984.

Quaker Faith and Practice (4th edition). Britain Yearly Meeting, 2009.

Rose, June. *Prison Pioneer: the story of Elizabeth Fry*. The History Press, 2007.

Skidmore, Gil. *Strength in Weakness: Writings of Eighteenth-Century Quaker Women*. Altmira Press, 2003.

Smith, Lynn. *Pacifists in Action: The experience of the Friends Ambulance Unit in the Second World War*

Walvin, James. *The Quakers: Money and Morals*. John Murray, 1998.

Woolman, John (edited by Philip Moulton). *The Journal and Major Essays of John Woolman*. Friends United Press, 2007.

INDEX